THE SUPEREST

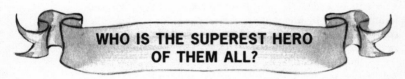

WHO IS THE SUPEREST HERO OF THEM ALL?

Kevin Cornell and Matthew Sutter

REBEL BASE

REBEL BASE BOOKS
CITADEL PRESS
Kensington Publishing Corporation
www.kensingtonbooks.com

REBEL BASE BOOKS are published by

Kensington Publishing Corp.
119 West 40th Street
New York, NY 10018

All Kensington titles, imprints, and distributed lines are
available at special quantity discounts for bulk purchases
for sales promotions, premiums, fund-raising, educational,
or institutional use. Special book excerpts or customized
printings can also be created to fit specific needs. For
details, write or phone the office of the Kensington special
sales manager: Kensington Publishing Corp., 119 West 40th
Street, New York, NY 10018, attn: Special Sales Department;
phone 1-800-221-2647.

First printing: January 2010

10 9 8 7 6 5 4 3 2 1

Printed in the United States of America

Library of Congress Control Number: 2009930448

ISBN-13: 978-0-8065-3135-9
ISBN-10: 0-8065-3135-5

6918

THE SUPEREST

Our heartfelt thanks go out to Mr. Andy Havens, who created the initial My Team vs. Your Team rules on which The Superest is based. Feel free to visit him at www.tinkerex.com for more great ideas.

FOREWORD

Hello.

Some of you may or may not remember me. My name is Hubert Perkins. I was quality assurance manager at Continental Battery Manufacturing in Sparks, Maryland, up until October 16, 2007.

That was the fateful day when I realized something important . . . the world had no superhero. And it needed one.

Someone to right the wrongs and wrong the rights. Someone for children to look up to, or down upon, depending on the height of the hero or, conversely, the child. Someone to pose for statues, and melt them down with their super-hot eye beams. So, removing my tie and wrapping it about my head, I stood on my desk, unlaced my shoe, and declared myself the world's first super-hero: The Unopposinator.

My power? I win every battle provided I have absolutely no opposition. Of course, later that day some shut-in from Long Island challenged me to a duel and I immediately forfeited. Nevertheless, for a brief shining moment, I was champion of the world.

Little did I know that my heroic act of cowardice would start a chain reaction, as superhero after superhero from around the globe arose to vie for the title of Current Champ.

We didn't really understand where we came from. It seem like one day a hero appeared with a certain power. And the next day, another hero appeared with a power that just happened to beat the previous person. Odd.

When the authors of this book asked me to write the forward, I jumped on the chance. Not just for the $25.00 gift certificate to Corndog Palace, but also because I have to admit—I miss my superhero past. I couldn't pass up the opportunity to once again partake in the dangerous dance, in some capacity. And I am not alone in this desire. Many of us who at one time wore the crown, dream to once again make a bid for the top.

Why, just the other day I was having lunch with Ron Whelp, an old friend of mine, who fought as The Termite back in January of 2008. I had just finished my corndog and gave him my leftover stick to gnaw on

when just out of the blue he says, "Hubert, I'm thinking of getting back in the game."

"Ronny," I said, "You can't handle that. You've had five pulp-induced heart attacks and countless bouts of varnish poisoning."

"Well," he says, "Maybe I'll just steer clear of that dining room furniture. Stick to lighter fare. Something organic, like Shaker furniture. Or maybe just paper."

"Bah," I said, "You'll never stick to a diet."

I guess this kind of hurt Ronny's feelings, because he stood up ran out of the place crying. Didn't even finish his toothpicks. But as I sat there, alone, the irresistible urge to superhero again suddenly awoke in my heart. My eyes gazed at his empty chair, confidence and adrenaline racing throughout my veins in equal parts. I pictured my non-opponent, not sitting there and posing absolutely no challenge. This fight was going to be a piece of cake.

I loosened my tie. And for one brief moment . . . I was, again, the Unnopposinator!

Then the waiter came and I got scared and put my shoe back on.

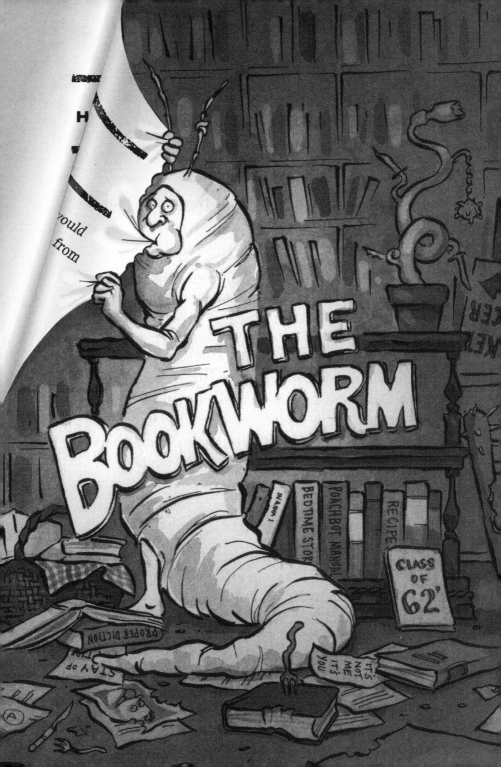

The Bookworm

POWER:

Ingests books.

NOTES: He used to fight as The Termite, but after his well-publicized defeat on the internet, he decided to try his hand in publishing. As it turns out, eating books is much easier on aging gums, and is generally a better way to antagonize a villain. Especially if you eat his diary.

Early Bird

POWER:

Can catch and eat any worm.

NOTES: He also has super-punctuality . . . but that impresses very few people. On the plus side, it gives him time to stretch and do some squat thrusts before a fight. Superheroes tend to have very tight hamstrings. It really makes a difference.

Cage Match

POWER:

Easily captures and contains the hungriest of birds.

NOTES: This sort of bizarrely disfigured hero is usually the result of a botched science experiment. Although this guy is just the result of a really effed-up Science Fair project.

Locke Smith

POWER:

Has a key for every lock.

NOTES: He even has the key to your heart. You like long twilight walks, right? And puppies? How do you feel about extremely cold metal hands?

Swing King

POWER:

His smooth manner and sexy harem persuades the most prudent hero to join his key party.

NOTES: Locke Smith exchanged every last key for one magical night. And about thirteen different STDs. And some unresolved paternity suits. You know, in retrospect, maybe it wasn't all that magical.

Censorion

POWER:

Eliminates all eroticism with clever censoring.

NOTES: Remember that baseball card with the dirty word on the bottom of the bat? He totally devalued that box set by $100.00.

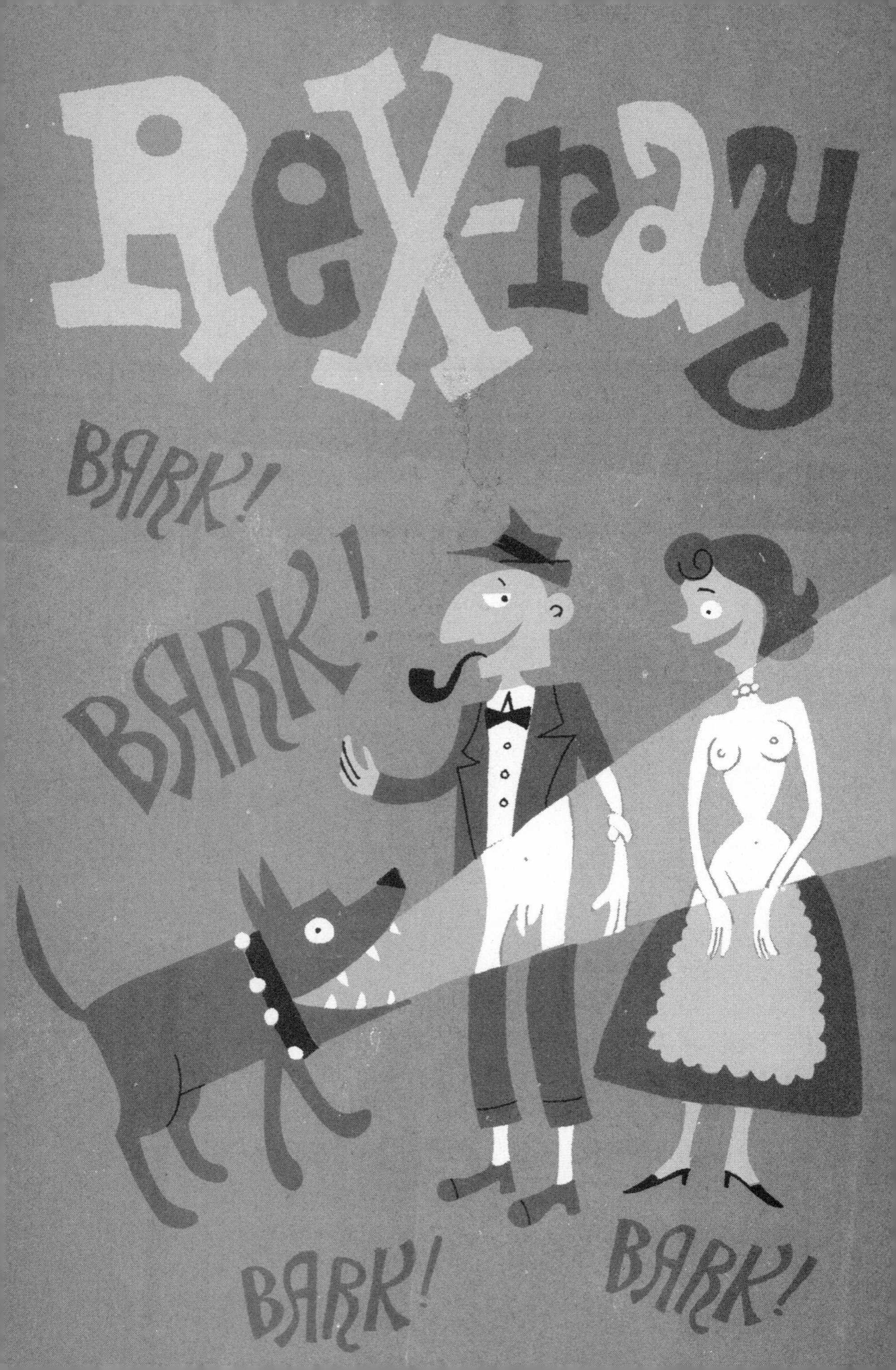
Rex-ray
BARK!
BARK!
BARK!
BARK!

Rex-ray

POWER:

His powerful bark is an X-ray beam.

NOTES: Positive selling point for potential owners: This cute little fella has been neutered. Negative selling point: After owning him for a couple days you'll probably end up sterile as well.

Poisoned Homework

POWER:

Possesses potent pooch-poisoning pages.

NOTES: For the first time ever, Rex-ray's owner will have a legitimate excuse for why his homework isn't done. Because he had to go to his dog's funeral.

Fold Man Chu

POWER:

The fastest and most lethal origami master in the world.

NOTES: Legend speaks of an ancient monk who dwells in a hidden monastery, defended by giant paper swans whose wings flap when you pull their tails.

Frostbite

POWER:

Nips fingers off with his ice-cold teeth.

NOTES: Rest assured, being frozen with fear is *not* due to the temperature. Unless you're watching horror movies at an Antarctic drive-in. In which case, how did you get your car there?

Doorman & Stringboy

POWER:

An indomitable tooth-yanking strategy.

NOTES: Did you hear that slam? That's the sound of justice being served. Did you hear that second slam? That was probably justice leaving early because it has a long commute home.

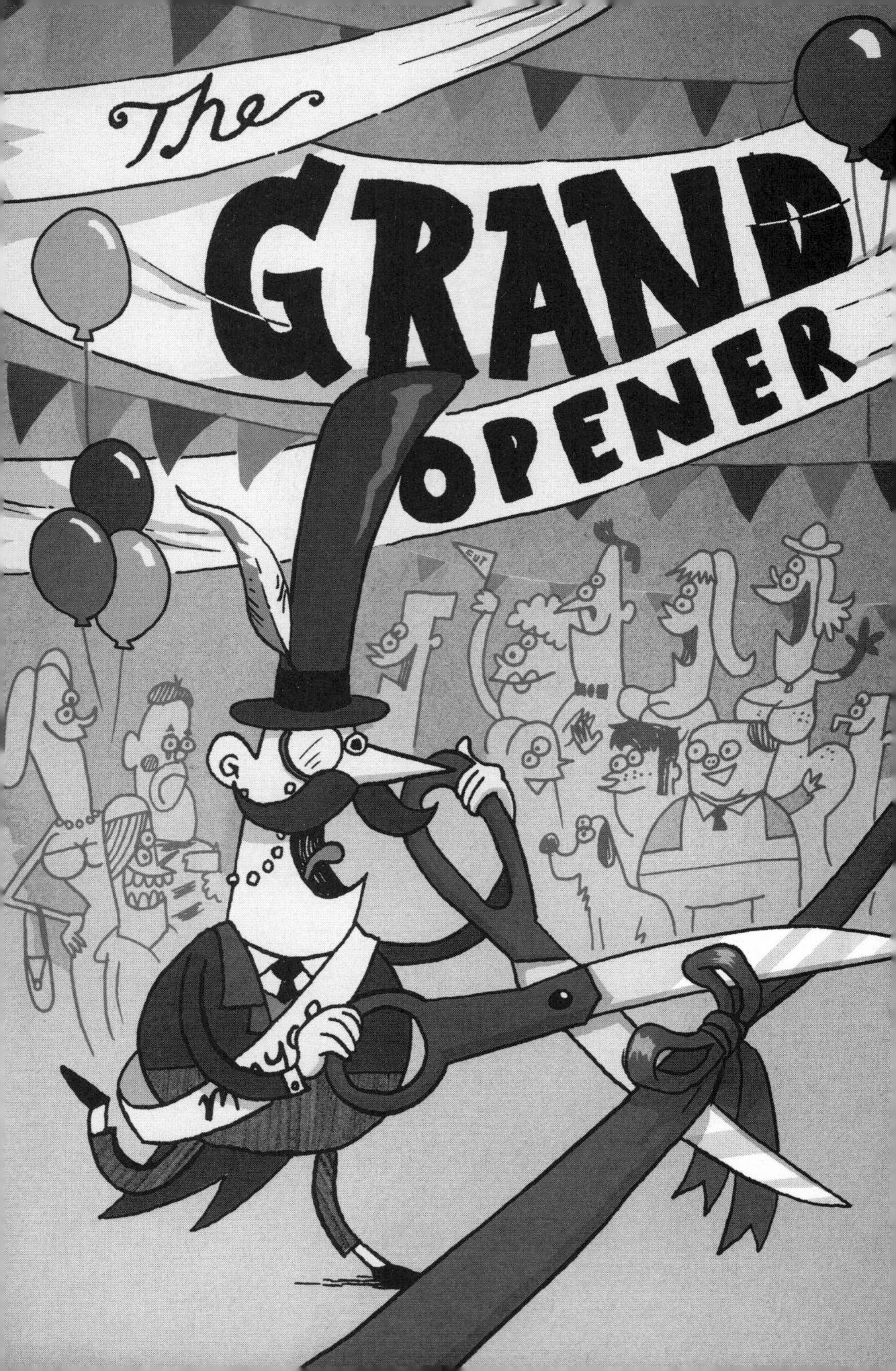
The
GRAND
OPENER

The Grand Opener

POWER:

Razor-sharp giant novelty scissors.

NOTES: Twine, ropes, ribbons . . . if it can be snipped, he'll do it. Doubly so if it spans a doorway. And triply so if he gets to give a speech beforehand.

The Spanish Bull

POWER:

Chases people through the streets.

NOTES: As it turns out, your mother was right—running with scissors really is dangerous. Come to think of it . . . she was right about avoiding bulls too. She gave good advice. You probably shouldn't have stuck her in that home.

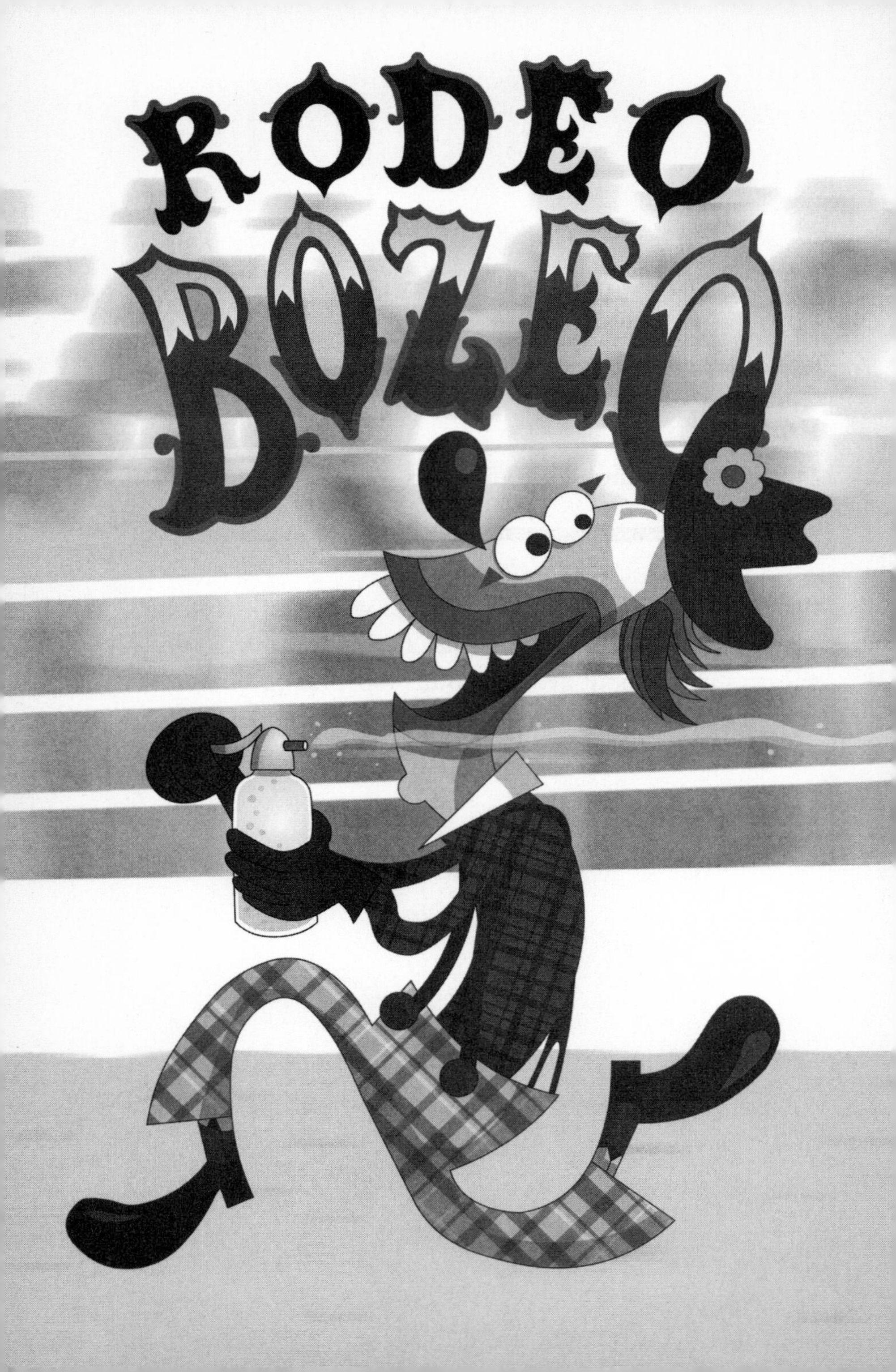
RODEO
BOZEO

Rodeo Bozeo

POWER:

Distracts bulls with his clever and whimsical cavorting.

NOTES: He got straight H.A.'s at Clown College. Good ol' Laffter U. Name one other university that can fit their entire enrollment in a single car.

Cold Cream Pieman

POWER:

Bakes cosmetic-removing pies.

NOTES: In the baking world these things are called "de-clowners." Everywhere else they're referred to as "the most horrible pie I've ever tasted."

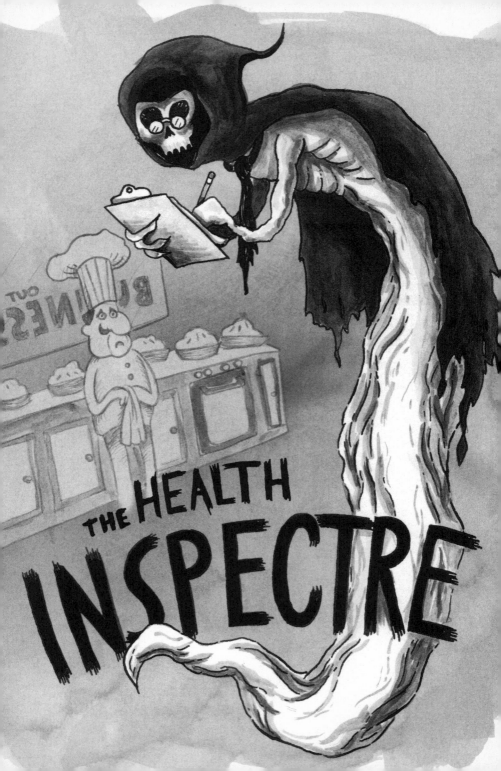

The Health Inspectre

POWER:

Shuts down restaurants, butcher shops, bars, and bakeries.

NOTES: He's quite good, but difficult to get a hold of. Your best bet is to have a coven of witches make a sacrifice at his grave on the stroke of midnight on the anniversary of his murder. His secretary will appear and schedule an appointment.

Exorcyst

POWER:

Malignantly destroys ghosts.

NOTES: He hears a lot of confessions along the lines of "Bless me father, for I think you're gross." But on the bright side, he's permanently excused from soup kitchen duties.

Lancer Lots

POWER:

Lances any sort of pus-filled sac. Eww.

NOTES: The hundred pounds of armor he wears is just so none of that vile liquid gets on him. And that quest for the Holy Grail was so he'd have something to throw up in afterward.

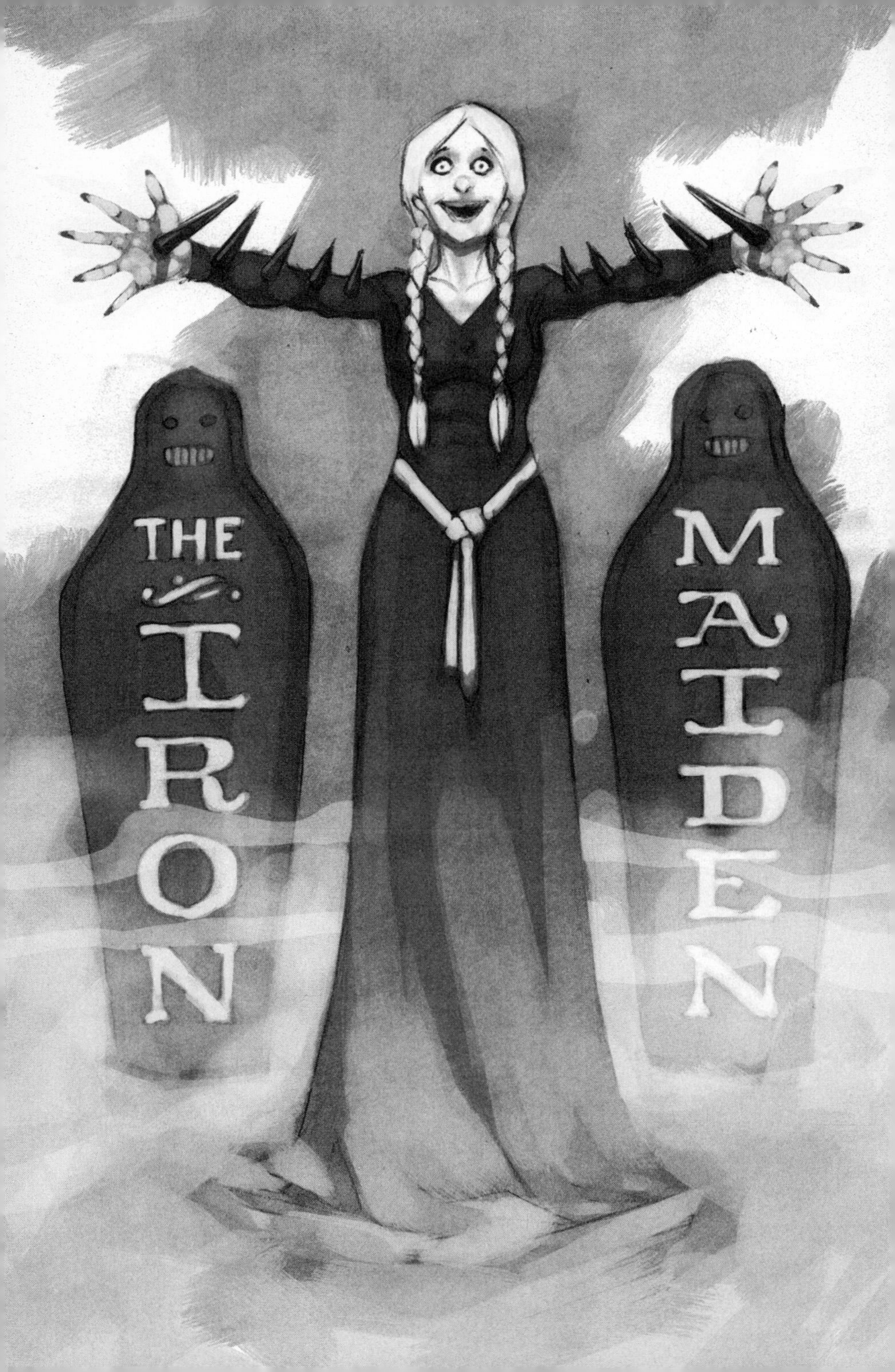
THE
IRON
MAIDEN

Iron Maiden

POWER:

Her seductive embrace pierces the soul. As well as armor, flesh, and—apparently—common sense.

NOTES: If only Lancer Lots wasn't such a sucker for distressed damsels, he might have remained unpunctured. It's not like she was in any real danger at the top of that tower, either. Except maybe from altitude sickness.

PetriFred

POWER:

His stone heart is unpierceable. And . . . the rest of him
is, too.

NOTES: His powers of stand-stillatude are unrivaled.
He had a brief affair with a bust of Cleopatra but broke
it off when he realized that her bust didn't include her
bust.

Sinmate

POWER:

Smashes, bashes, crushes, and cracks rocks.

NOTES: Parent Rocks scare their children with stories about how the one-man chain gang will pummel them to sand if they don't behave.

Parole Piranha & Rehabiligator

POWER:

Help prisoners escape from a life of prison. Then later, the prison of life.

NOTES: The key to dodging conviction is to earn the jury's sympathy, which is pretty easy when you force your clients to give testimony while they simmer in a vat of water with onions and carrots.

Salt Shaker

Salt Shaker

POWER:

Blessed with Thine gift of Superior Saltiness.

NOTES: His diligent and pious oversalting of freshwater habitats has put Parole Piranha and Rehabiligator on the fast track to extinction. Brotherly love doesn't extend to other species, apparently.

The Practical Joker

POWER:

Serious pranking skills.

NOTES: He actually only knows one prank . . . you know . . . that one where you screw the head off the saltshaker? He finds it hilarious.

Five Card Studs (no wilds)

POWER:

Entertain at parties, get-togethers, and casinos.

NOTES: These guys just won't allow jokers to join the fun. Except the "beating jokers in the face" type of fun. But not any of the gyrating or hip-thrusting fun. Unless that's in the face as well.

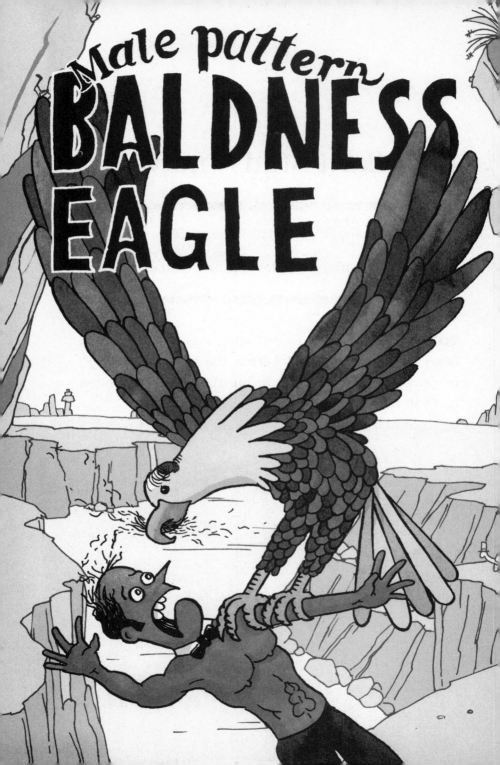

Male Pattern Baldness Eagle

POWER:

Plucks the hairs from men's heads to make a fantastic nest.

NOTES: His insecurities and need for building materials are making men with full heads of hair an endangered species.

Poach Pals

POWER:

Three great friends who each need three great eagle parts.

NOTES: You won't find a closer-knit group. By which we mean that these three are good friends, as opposed to them being three people with a common interest in knitting who live in close proximity to one another. Even though they are that as well.

Love Triangulator

POWER:

Ruins friendships with sexual tension.

NOTES: One minute you're the best of friends, the next you're caught up in series of carefully crafted, sexy misunderstandings. Nothing is more uneven than isosceles love.

The Cornerer

POWER:

Adds corners with needle, thread, and impunity.

NOTES: He once turned a triaugmented triangular prism into a gyroelongated square dipyramid. It was enough to make you puke!

HayteStack

POWER:

Makes it impossible for anyone to find a needle in his grassy layers.

NOTES: In the fall he gives rides at the orchard when he teams up with Tractorasaur. Parties of four or more get a free pumpkin! (Under 10 pounds, limit one per customer.)

NeanderThawed

POWER:

"Me bang rocks. Make tiny lightning. Burn hay."

NOTES: Discovered in a glacier, NeanderThawed was unfrozen and now uses his fascination with fire to fight evil 10,000 years in the future. Things like a mastodon robbing a bank. Or a giant sloth that parks in a handicap space. Though . . . actually, that's probably legal.

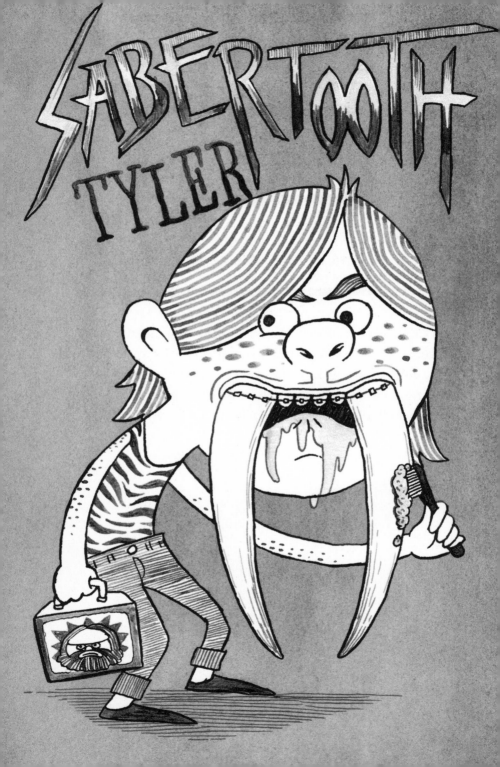

Sabertooth Tyler

POWER:

Sports a magnificent pair of Saber Teeth and a lust for caveman blood.

NOTES: His father was a tiger, and his mother was a museum curator. Together they conceived a child whose preternatural hunger for prehistoric flesh knows no bounds!

Dr. Van Helstink

POWER:

Substandard vampire-hunting skills.

NOTES: Van Helstink (Ph.D., Dpl., Lpd., Dop., etc.) appears to have a doctorate in everything but dentistry, which is a shame, because he really should learn the difference between saber teeth and fangs.

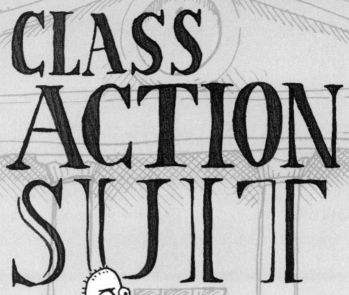

CLASS ACTION SUIT

Class Action Suit

POWER:

Puts doctors out of business.

NOTES: A finely tailored Super Suit like this vastly compounds Litigation Power. No doctor stands a chance. Especially if all 34 of that doctor's degrees turn out to be honorary.

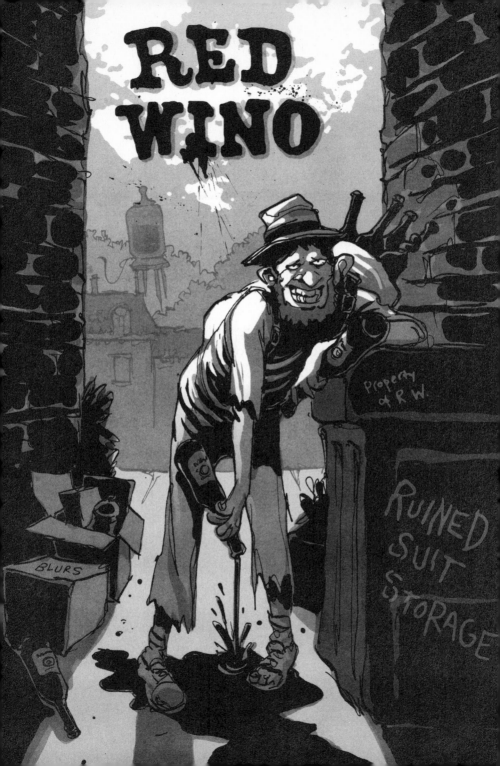

Red Wino

POWER:

Ruins suits permanently.

NOTES: The only thing he can't stain is his soul. Because it's so difficult to masturbate with those fingerless hobo gloves on.

Tramp Trap

POWER:

Sends hobos to that great freight car in the sky.

NOTES: No hobo can resist a Frigidaire estate with reinforced corrugation and power flaps, plus a secret compartment for polka-dotted bindles on sticks.

PACK RAT
discarded "cute-animal" hair
DISCARDED HORSE HEAD (and human head)
UNUSED BLURS
BLACK MARKET ITEMS (slightly skewered)
UNUSED DEODOR-EYES
UP
THIS SIDE UP
RUBBER ANVILS

Pack Rat

POWER:

Overstuffs cardboard boxes with packing material.

NOTES: Tramp Trap doesn't look too good. He seems to be having trouble breathing. Wait, do boxes breathe? Foxes do, but similar spelling doesn't necessarily indicate similar respiratory habits.

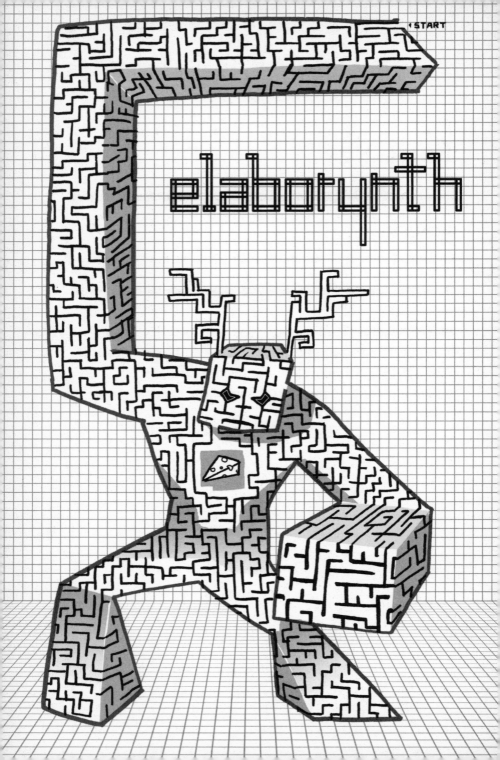

Elaborynth

POWER:

Rodents get lost in his ever-changing maze of limbs.

NOTES: He's the most popular hero on children's place mats and the backs of cereal boxes. If you defeat him you get your choice of cheese!

The Spoiler

POWER:

Can cheat his way through any puzzle.

NOTES: He has never actually solved anything by himself. He starts mystery novels on the back page, rearranges the stickers on a Rubik's Cube™, and seems to win at Monopoly only when he's the "banker."

3rd Act Girlfriend

POWER:

Sacrifices her popularity to help nerds find their inner beauty.

NOTES: Such a perfect ending for both her and The Spoiler, as they learn to channel their respective obsessions into a mutually crippling sexual addiction that will leave little time for finding Warp Levels.

LATE PERIOD

Late Period

POWER:

Strains relationships to the point of breaking.

NOTES: Whoops . . . 3rd Act Girlfriend just became 1st Act Mother. Late Period is unusually chipper for a hero whose ability relies on being peed upon.

GRAMMAR POLICE.

Grammar Police

POWER:

Keep punctuation in line.

NOTES: They'll catch that tardy period. These are the same guys that arrested that double hyphen posing as an em dash. And that paragraph that hung all those quotes.

Soap Scum

POWER:

Prevents further exposure to ?!@!?!.

NOTES: A couple mouthwashes from this guy and kids will never utter another string of "Grammar Police." They might need to sleep with a nite-lite until they're eighteen or so, though.

(chamber)
ᵛ
MER MAID

Mer(Chamber)maid

POWER:

Removes Soap Scum. Even underwater!

NOTES: She can make an oyster bed in 30 seconds flat. Oh, and if you leave your towels floating in the Marianas Trench, she'll wash them for you.

Oil Derek

POWER:

Ruins the seas with his oil slicks.

NOTES: He's been on the lookout for an alternative resource for killing wildlife. There's been some discussion of corn-derived poisons, but scientists debate its sustainability and its notoriously low poison yield per hectare.

Ladle of the Lake

POWER:

Ladles unwanted materials from bodies of water.

NOTES: She used to be the Lady of the Lake, until that run-in with the Sword Swallower. Now the only royalty she can serve is chicken à la king.

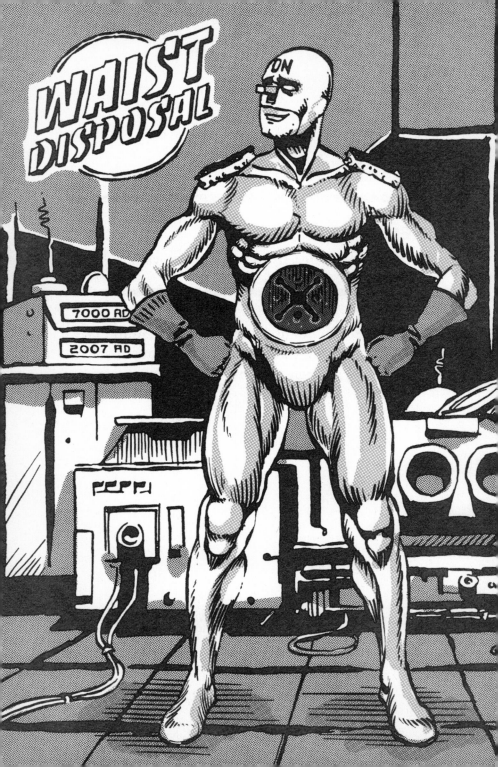

Waist Disposal

POWER:

Mangles utensils with his gnashing midsection.

NOTES: He used to work in the kitchen at the IHOP but the mulberry syrup kept gumming up his gears. Every couple months his stomach starts to smell a little funky, and he needs to pick a fight with The Orange-a-tang. After that he's citrus-fresh!

Auntie Acid

POWER:

Stills turbulent stomachs.

NOTES: They erected this big statue of her in the town square after she defeated Dr. Dyspepper. Oh, and remember that empty lot behind the Big Boy? They built a skate park! Radical!

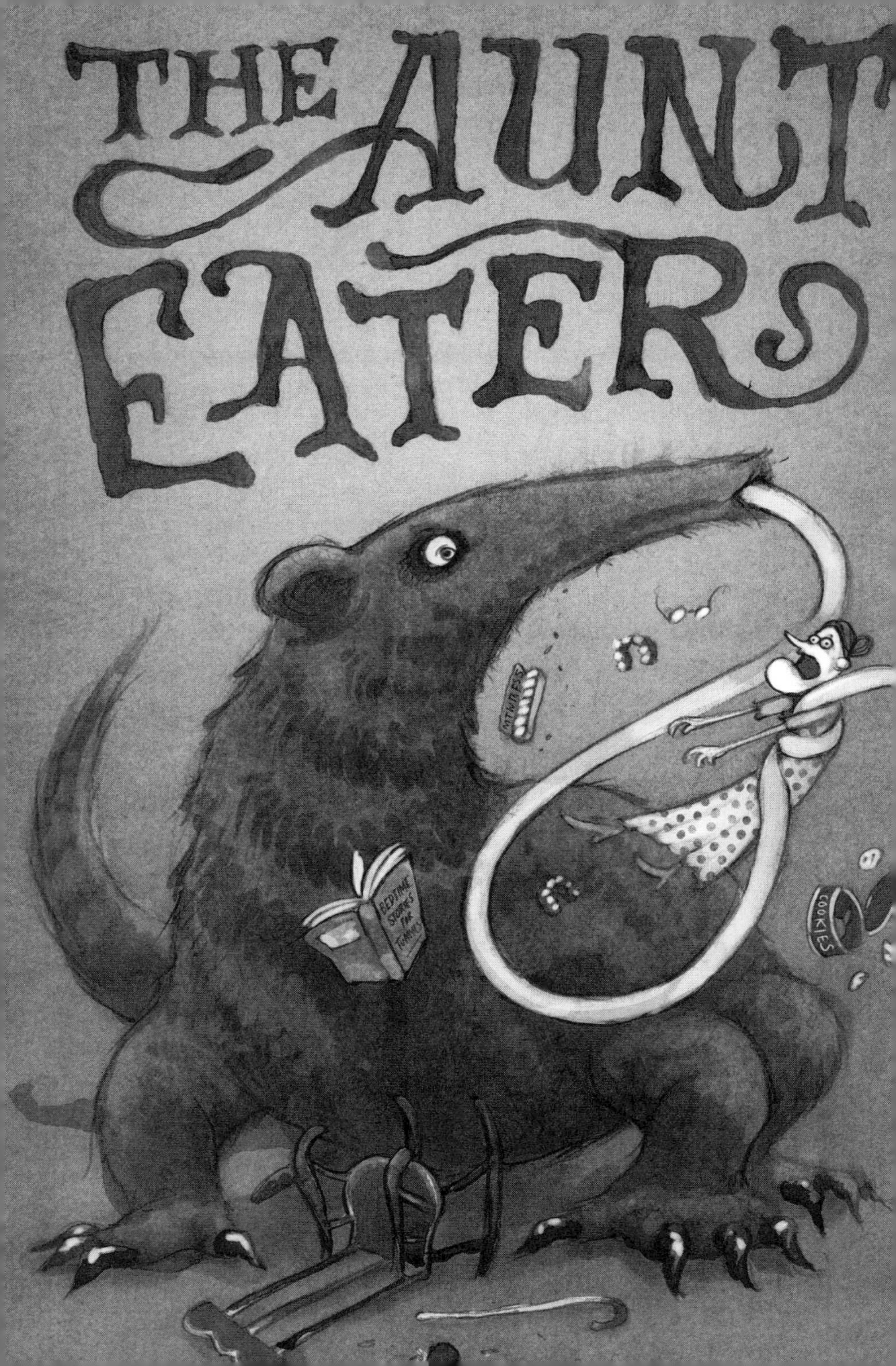
THE AUNT EATERS
BEDTIME STORIES FOR TUMMIES
COOKIES

The Aunt Eater

POWER:

Uses its giant tongue to snatch up and devour Aunts.

NOTES: Auntie Acid has a pleasant, fizzy taste. And she doesn't give you brain freeze, like Aunt Arctic did.

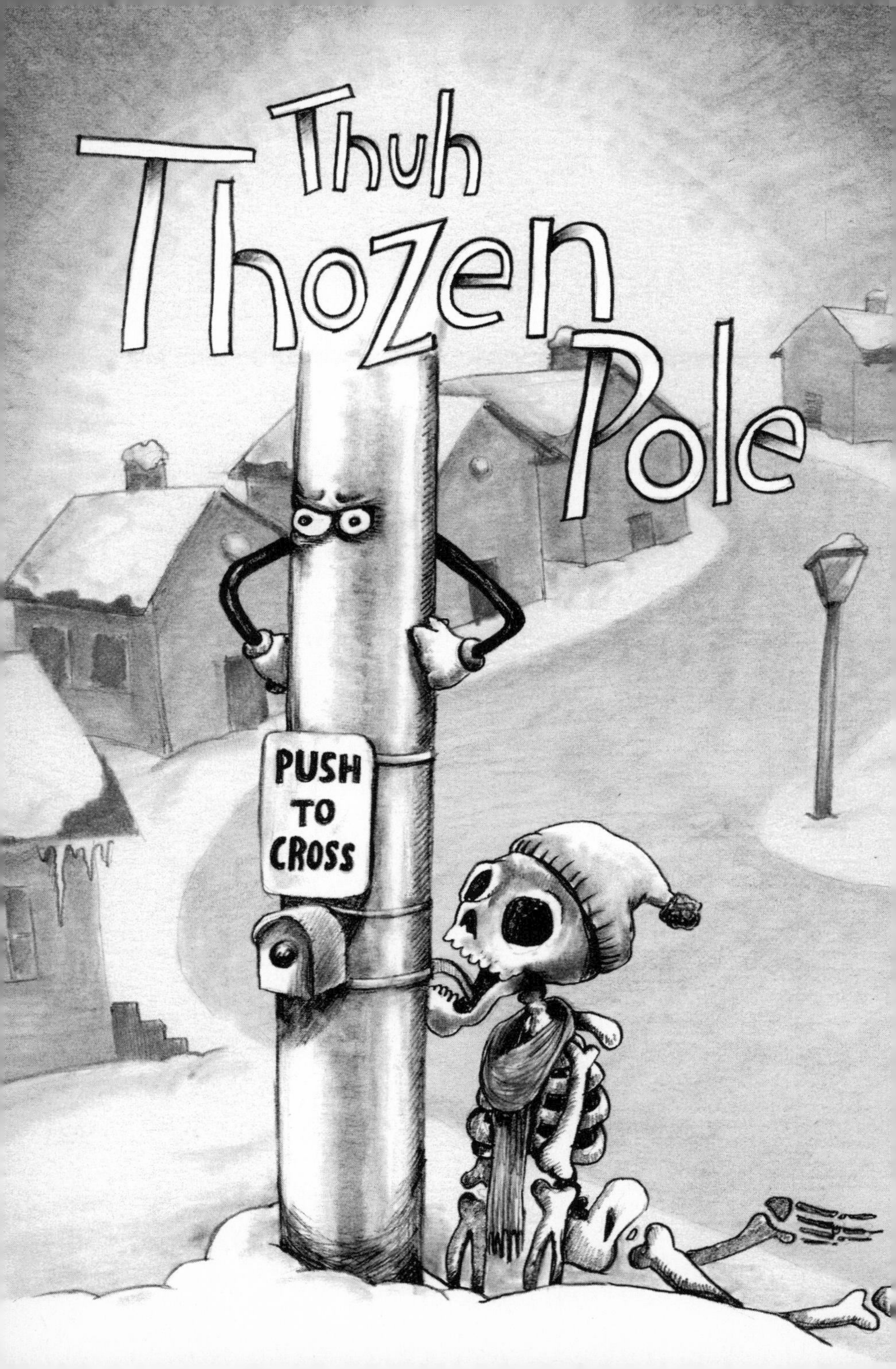
Thuh
Thozen Pole
PUSH TO CROSS

Thuh Thozen Pole

POWER:

Its frigid metal body is practically irresistible.

NOTES: He has a surprisingly large number of victims for a hero who can't move. Most of which are the result of double-dog dares.

Polly Petless

POWER:

Buries poles in flyers.

NOTES: No hero has yet to top that amazing act of skill and determination for which she will forever be immortalized: subletting that apartment between the two sewage treatment plants.

Gesundmight

POWER:

His powerful sneezes blow away all signage.

NOTES: He spent years working up an allergy to just about everything. He usually sneezes 4–6 times in a row, so please hold your "God bless you" until the end.

THE NAUGHTY KNOTTERS

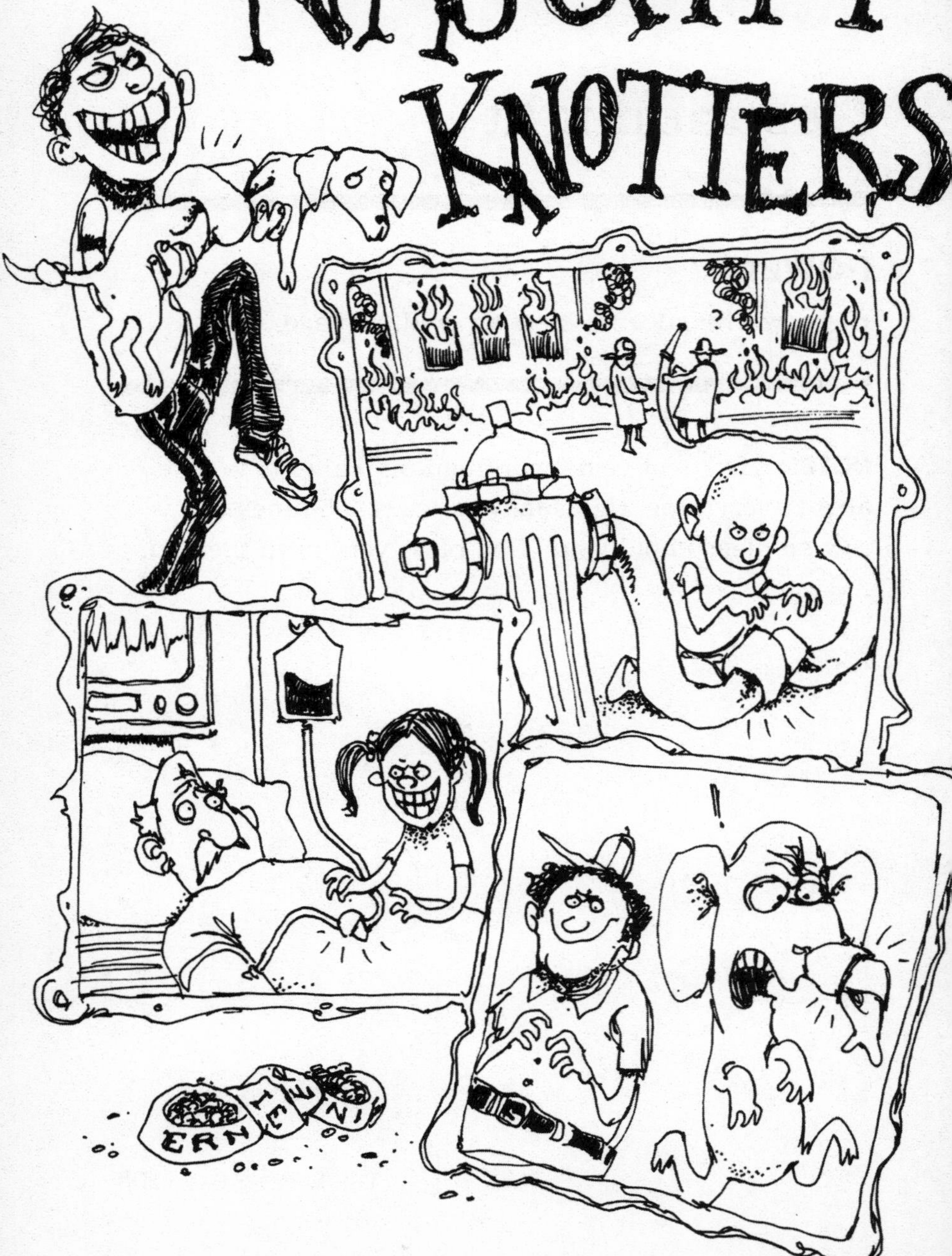

The Naughty Knotters

POWER:

Malicious knot-tying skills.

NOTES: These little brats would have been sentenced to juvee years ago, except they somehow tied the building in a sheep shank. If you're unfamiliar with buildings, this is a very difficult thing to do.

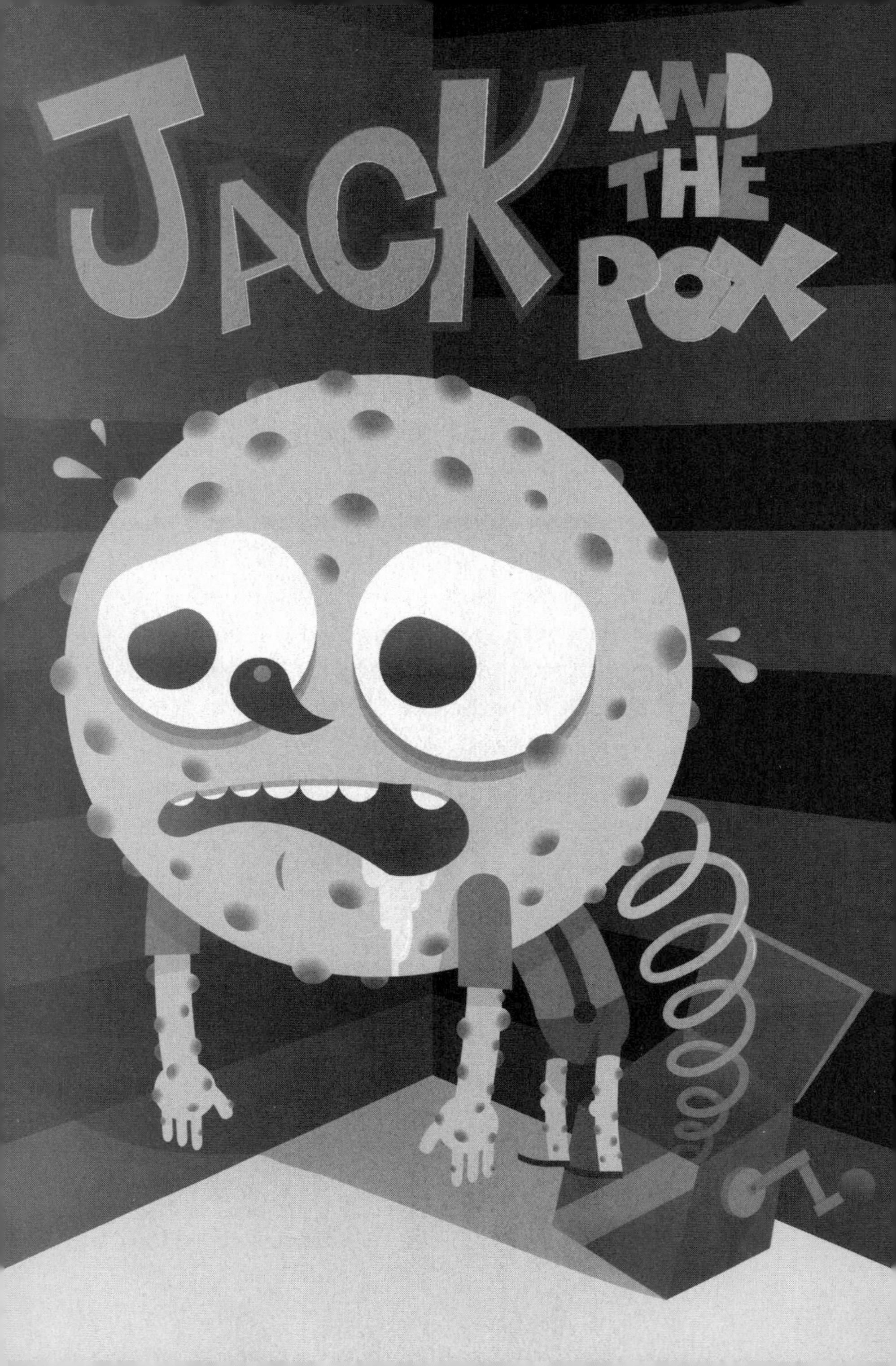
JACK AND THE POX

Jack and the Pox

POWER:

Condemns children to weeks of confinement and itching.

NOTES: Most people are aware of the consequences of opening him, but that delightful song is just too irresistible.

Quaranteam

POWER:

Secludes hazardous materials.

NOTES: It's so much safer to fight evil in an allergen-free environment. Though, to their detriment, when punching and kicking is left up to a committee vote, it makes for a superhero with very, very slow reflexes.

The Penetrator

POWER:

Wiggles his way into tight spots.

NOTES: He's had some impressive accomplices over the years . . . Ovulator Satyr, ZyGoat, The Panty Raider, Spring Break Snake, Girl Gone Wild, The Prom Knight. It's a veritable *Who's Who* of salacious supers.

Ty T. Whitey

POWER:

Raises temperatures to unbearable degrees.

NOTES: To be honest, the temperatures are just kind of uncomfortable for anyone dressed normally. But if you're the kind of idiot who builds your costume entirely out of latex and petroleum jelly, you deserve to smother.

UnderWereWolf

POWER:

Turns into a vicious half-man, half-wolf when exposed to underwear.

NOTES: He absolutely destroyed that Victoria's Secret fashion show last fall. And as for that JC Penney show, that was ruined before it started. One of the models used to be a dude.

Cloud Cannoneer

POWER:

Fires clouds from his Cannon of Positive Thinking.

NOTES: Normally clouds can't hurt anyone, but unfortunately for UnderWereWolf, all these have a silver lining.

Wind Chimera

POWER:

His musical breath blows clouds to the next zip code.

NOTES: On a hale and dread wind, out of the fog of myth, comes the beast of beasts whose unholy blowing heralds destruction! What? Why is everyone giggling?

SideSplitter

POWER:

Makes people and animals laugh so hard they divide.

NOTES: His cover charge is pretty affordable. People usually don't want to pay a lot of money to see a comic who will kill them. Unless there's a drink special.

BackRow Bully

POWER:

Produces his own ammunition for super-heckling.

NOTES: His presence is heralded by his heroic tagline: "You suck. Get off the stage!"

Transplantra

POWER:

Removes plants from inadequate vessels so that they can grow.

NOTES: No responsible gardener would expect tomatoes to grow in a smoky nightclub setting. Or in a head with such low nitrogen levels.

Guardin' Gnome

POWER:

Protects gardens.

NOTES: The daisy sector has the highest security clearance, but the pumpkin patch is pretty well guarded, too. All those impaled green thumbs lining the flagstone path will attest to that.

NarcoLeper

POWER:

His presence induces drowsiness in even the most stalwart of watchmen. And a little nausea.

NOTES: They say leprosy is difficult to catch. But I bet your chances increase greatly if you settle down for a long nap and some intimate spooning with a leper.

Upstairs Neighbor

POWER:

Can keep anyone awake, day or night.

NOTES: You can hit the ceiling with your broomstick as many times as you want—he's super-inconsiderate as well. Oh, great. He just started dating Yodeling Yvette.

The Librarian

POWER:

Her patented Shush-O-Ray keeps people from making noise.

NOTES: You might think that a librarian superhero would be too uptight to beat a villain to death with his own overdue book, but you'd be wrong. Your small-mindedness is her biggest foe.

The Illiterator

POWER:

Makes reading completely impossible.

NOTES: Won't be much need for super-librarians once no one can read. I doubt enjoy even   be able anyone will to   the.

crossword

puzzles

HOW TO PLAY ON YOUR OWN

Got a few superhero ideas in your head? Looking to start a Superest match of your own? Here are the simple rules of the game:

> *"One person draws a superhero with a power. The next person draws a superhero whose power defeats the first. Continue until someone's hand cramps up or brain dies."*

Of course, you probably already figured that out. But did you know that there are all sorts of variations on the game that can make things even more fun? Here are a few extra rules to try out on your own, or with some friends:

1. Limit your heroes to only one character archetype. For instance, Only Robots, or Only Monsters, or Only People Working in an Office.

2. Play with multiple people! There's no reason you need to go in the same sequence—or even limit the game to two artists—as long as you switch artists after each hero.

3. Give each hero some additional details. For instance, all the heroes must have a sidekick, or a utility belt, or perhaps a lair.

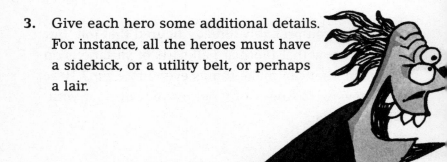

4. Use to spreadable draw pictures your and eat your masterpiece finished when you're.

5. Create a secret identity for the hero after the game is over.

condiments

TIPS ON CREATING YOUR OWN HERO

So you're having trouble creating a superhero, hmmmm? Well, here are a few tips to help you get started or break out of a rut:

1. Every hero's greatest strength can be turned into his or her worst weakness. For instance, a hero with Hammer Hands might always be able to beat a nail. But he could never beat a Giant Screw.

2. Sometimes it's helpful to think of the name, then create the hero. The best hero names are new twists on common phrases or names that use alliteration.

3. Superheroes love to have costumes. Add capes, masks, boots, gloves, emblems, utility belts, and weapons to make your hero look the part.

4. Superheroes work best when they've got one thing they do really well. Don't give your hero a bunch of different superpowers.

5. Another good starting point for a hero is deciding whether he's a good guy or bad guy; that often opens unforeseen avenues of superpowerdom!

6. Take a cue from supervillains. If you can't beat a

hero's power, you can always threaten something or someone really _____ to them. Kidnap their dog!

important

7.   Not every hero has to have a clever title. Feel free to name after your hero family, _____, or things you see on while the floor you're drawing.

members

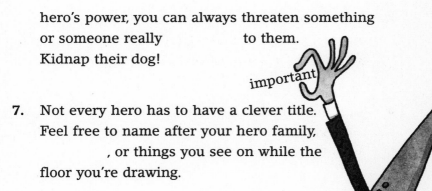

READING GROUP GUIDE

1. How does Cornell's depiction of gender neutral superheroes contrast with modern theories of the hermaphroditic ideal?

2. Does Sutter's deviation from traditional foot anatomy foreshadow evolutionary eventualities, or is it reactionary propaganda against metatarsal autonomy?

3. In many ways, the struggle between Late Period and Grammar Police reflects the broader struggle between different social classes in punctuation. Discuss.

4. In what ways do the powers of Rex-Ray and Jack in the Pox challenge established philosophies of Western medicine and/or logic?

5. What were the advantages enjoyed by Swing King that allowed him to overcome Locke Smith but left him susceptible to defeat by Censorion? How could these advantages be rented out at a modest price from the website www.swingkingescorts.com by lonely men ages 18–65 like yourself?

6. Elaborynth is an actual, solvable maze. Discuss. Or solve. Whichever you think you can do without destroying the book.

7. In what ways do the stereotypes portrayed by Red Wino damage the wino community in a global sense and simultaneously threaten domestic bindle production?

8. In way what Sutter's Mexico hero sexual frustration have octopus los fifteenth century?

represent

9. The Naughty Knotters struck several other heroes, though not fatally. Identify the victims and win a prize! Not from us, but we're sure someone will give you something.